# Stay Safe!

## Claire Llewellyn

QED Publishing

First published in the UK in 2006 by
QED Publishing
A Quarto Group company
226 City Road
London EC1V 2TT
www.qed-publishing.co.uk

A catalogue record for this book is available from the British Library.

ISBN 1 84538 370 2

Written by Claire Llewellyn
Designed by Susi Martin
Editor Louisa Somerville
Consultant Ruth Miller B.Sc., M.I.Biol., C.Biol.
Illustrations John Haslam
Photographs Michael Wicks

Publisher Steve Evans
Editorial Director Jean Coppendale
Art Director Zeta Davies

Printed and bound in China

**Picture credits**

Key: t = top, b = bottom, c = centre, l = left, r = right, FC = front cover

**Gettyimages** Zen Sekizawa 16.
**Corbis** LWA-Dann Tardif/Corbis 4, / Jouval Frederique/Corbis Sygma 14.

Words in **bold** are explained
in the glossary on page 22.

# Contents

You
can
do it!

When you were a baby, your parents did everything for you. They helped to keep you safe.

Now that you're older, you can begin to take care of yourself.

Star tip

As you grow, it's important to look after your body and keep it safe.

How did these things help to keep you safe when you were a baby?

stair gate

cot

playpen

safety harness

# Do it!

Find photos of yourself doing things, such as singing, swimming, reading and eating. Choose some to make a poster that shows how brilliant your body is and what it can do.

# Home, sweet home

We spend lots of time at home. It's a place where we feel safe.

Did you know that some things around the house might harm you? It's important to take care.

**Quick quiz!**

Which of these things can be dangerous? Which help to keep us safe?

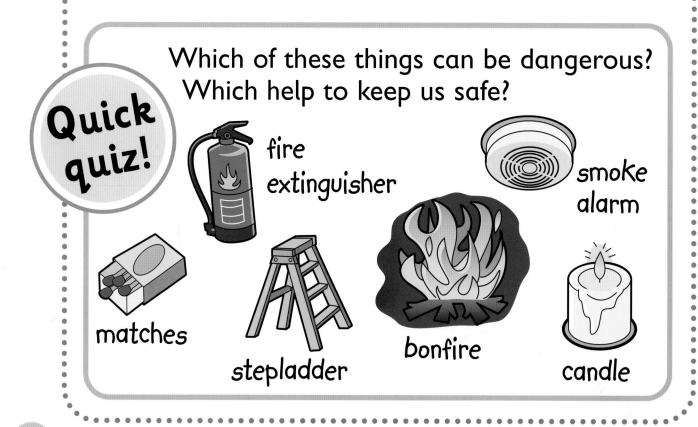

fire extinguisher

smoke alarm

matches

stepladder

bonfire

candle

# Electricity

Electricity is a kind of power that can be very **dangerous.** Televisions, computers, DVD players and lamps run on electricity. NEVER play with electric **plugs, sockets, lightbulbs** or wires.

Safety first!

- Don't play on the stairs. It is easy to slip and fall.

- Never lean out of upstairs windows. It's a long way to the ground!

- Fire is hot and dangerous. Never play with matches or candles, or go near an open fire.

## Do it!

Draw a sign that warns people of danger. What could it look like? What colour should it be? Place it near something at home that you think could be a danger.

# Careful in the kitchen!

We spend lots of time in the kitchen. It's where food is kept and cooked.

Take care when someone is cooking. Stay away from the hot oven and from pans that are on the top.

**Watch out!**

## Knives and scissors

Many kitchen tools, such as knives and scissors, are very sharp. They are good for cutting and chopping food. Don't touch them or you could cut yourself!

## Quick quiz!

steam iron

mug of tea

hot soup

toaster

## Do it!

Cooking with a grown-up is a good way to learn about safety in the kitchen. Do you know how to peel a potato? Can you **grate** some cheese?

# Bathroom bothers

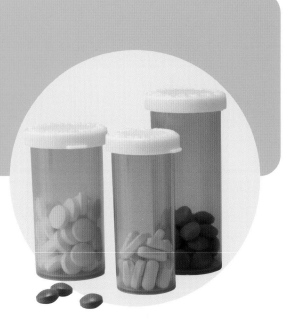

We use the bathroom to brush our teeth, use the toilet or have a bath.

Some medicines look like sweets. NEVER try to eat them.

We also keep **medicines** there. Medicines help us to feel better when we are ill.

## Watch out!

### Medicines

Medicines can be dangerous. If you need medicine, an adult must give it to you. Never take it on your own.

Wet baths and floors are slippery – take care, or you could get a nasty bump.

Water can be so hot that it can burn your skin. Always test the water before you get into a bath.

Never sniff or swallow things that are used to clean the bathroom. They could make you sick and harm your body.

What can you *see* in this bathroom that could hurt you?

# Road safety

We all need to use roads, but it's important to learn how to stay safe.

Cars, bikes and trucks are heavy and fast. What could happen if one hit you?

**Watch out!**

## On the pavement

When you walk along roads, stay on the pavement and keep away from the **kerb**. Walk close to the adult you are with. Keep your eyes and ears open.

**Star tip**

When you go out at night, try to wear or carry something white or that glows. Then drivers can see you in the dark.

How do these help to keep people safe on the road?

car seat

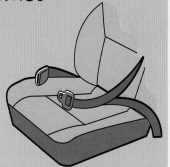
cycling helmet

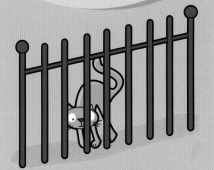
street railings

day-glow harness

seat belt

## Do it!

Some people drive too fast. Make a sign that warns drivers to slow down. What picture would you put on it? What would your sign say?

Your friend wants to play football on the pavement. What do you do?

**Think about it!**

# Safe crossings

Sometimes we have to cross the road. This can be tricky and needs a lot of care.

Always use **pedestrian crossings**. They are the safest places to cross the road.

Safety first!

## Pedestrian crossings

There are three kinds of pedestrian crossing:
- school crossing
- zebra crossing
- pelican crossing

These are all good places to cross the road.

# Crossing the road

- Never cross the road by yourself.
- Wait until a grown-up tells you it is safe to cross.
- Walk across the road quickly. Do not run.
- Keep your eyes and ears open for traffic.

**Think about it!**

You want to cross the road. Who can help you?

15

# Playing safe

It's good fun going to the playground with your friends!

Take care while you're having fun. It's easy to get hurt – and to hurt others, too.

**Safety first!**

- A roundabout spins very fast. Don't jump on or off until it stops.

- Swings are heavy and hard to stop. Don't get in their way.

- Take care on ladders and climbing frames. If you slip, it's a long way to fall!

- Move away from the bottom of the slide. The next person could whizz down fast.

A friend dares you to jump off the roundabout while it's still moving. What do you do?

Always use playground equipment sensibly. It's the best way to keep yourself and others safe.

**Search and find!**

Can you spot any dangers in this playground picture?

# Water warning!

It's fun to play in water on a warm summer's day. But water can be very dangerous.

Take care when you play in it.

**Watch out!**

## Water

Fish can live and breathe in water, but people can't.

If you are under water, you will need to get to the **surface** quickly to breathe in more air.

## Do it!

Go to the swimming pool every week. This will help you feel at home in water and you will soon learn how to swim.

- Stay away from rivers, lakes and ponds unless you're with an adult.

- Never paddle or swim without an adult being near.

- Don't jump on or duck your friends at the swimming pool.

## Think about it!

You are playing in a garden with your friend when your ball lands in the pond. What do you do?

- Be very careful when playing in paddling pools.

## Quick quiz!

Where do you see these? How do they help to keep people safe?

arm bands

life guard

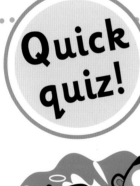

float

life jacket

# Out and about

Who keeps you safe when you're out and about – Mum, Dad or another grown-up?

Stay close to them. If you don't, you could get lost and that can be scary.

## Do it!

Learn your address and home phone number. If you get lost, this will help someone to contact your family.

- Strangers are people you don't know. Don't talk to strangers.

- Never take sweets from strangers or go anywhere with them.

- Don't stroke strange dogs. If one comes up to you, stand still and wait for it to go away.

**Star tip** Make sure a parent or another grown-up always knows where you are.

**Watch out!**

# I'm lost!

What should you do if you get lost? Ask for help right away – from a person such as a police officer or shop assistant.

This will help you to stay safe.

# Glossary

**dangerous** something that can cause you harm

**equipment** the slides, see-saw and other games in a playground

**grate** to cut things into small shreds, using a grater

**kerb** the edge between a pavement and a road

**lightbulb** a glass globe which gives out light when electricity passes through it

**medicine** the special liquid or tablets that we take to make us feel better when we are ill

**pedestrian crossing** a safe place to cross the road for a person who is walking

**plug** the plastic and metal part at the end of an electric cable that fits into a socket

**socket** a special hole into which a plug fits to make something electrical work. A socket is usually on a wall

**surface** the top or outside of anything

# Index

# Notes
## for parents and teachers

- Look at photographs with your children of when they were babies. Ask your children to look for any safety equipment (e.g. reins, playpen) or other ways in which they were protected.

- Discuss safety in the kitchen. Ask your children to suggest which places in the kitchen could be dangerous. Look at a variety of kitchen tools. Show the children what they are made of and the different jobs they can do.

- Ask the children to suggest all the things that could be hot in their homes. Draw pictures and label each one. Discuss the different ways children can avoid getting burnt.

- Help your children to make a list of the electrical machines they have in their homes. Ask them to show the list to their grandparents. How many of the items did they have in their house when they were young? Did they look/work the same?

- Visit a park or playground with your children. What safety measures are in place? Why? Discuss how accidents could happen in the playground and what steps the children can take to prevent them.

- Next time you are walking along the road with your children, discuss the best places to cross the road. Encourage them to keep their eyes and ears open. Can they spot any dangers?

- Invite a road crossing patrol into school and interview him/her about road safety. What kind of uniform does the patrol wear?

- Discuss with your children how shiny things reflect the light and keep us safe in the dark. Investigate reflective strips and other shiny surfaces. How and where would they expect them to shine? Try out your children's ideas to find out if they were right.

- Ask your children to think of animals that can breathe under water (or hold their breath for a very long time). Using books and the Internet, research one of these animals and write a fact sheet about it.

- Help the children to list all the different places they regularly go to together – e.g. the library, park, swimming pool. Talk about what they would do if they got lost in each of these places. Who could they ask for help?